LOST AND FOUND

PRACHI MAHAJAN

Throughout life, we tend to morph and alter counting on

The things we tend to see and therefore the experiences we tend to exchange.

Writing has been my refuge while usurping the little battlefields of adolescents.

So I provide to you,

The beating heart of the numerous tiny battles

I have felt desirous to conquer in Some way

Contents

Contents

Preface

Lost and found is a book that you can always go back to. It's a book that will make you feel, act, and see things differently. You will feel the hit of every emotion, the sadness, the joy, the suffering. It's a book that will make you feel everything. It's a book you can relate to.

It's a book about conquering different battles of life. This book will give you a positive outlook towards life.

Life is really a lost treasure. It's not always what you expect but we have our share of good and bad. Each one a us has such a memory, the sweet-sour taste of life that still lingers in our mind. It is a collection of poetry and prose.

CHAPTER ONE

EMBRACING YOURSELF

Daisies growing from the rugged lines of her skin.
Lavender flourishing from the corners of her flaws.
Nightshade petals bleeding across her bruised lips,
Thorns producing atop her fingertips.
Vines of wild tangling themselves inside her lungs and organs;
With roses nestling in the contours of her Collarbones.
Dandelions sprouting from her many scars.
And, Sunflowers weaving in her scalp like the strands Of her hair.
Seedlings of oak trees spread in her toes.
For she is a garden,
An incredible rarity of beauty.

When I was born into this world, I wasn't told right away that I'm supposed to dress in a particular way because I belong to a particular gender.

When we're born, we're equal, each one of us, irrespective of our caste, religion, gender, and race. We have two pairs of limbs, a face with eyes, nose, and lips.

We're not aliens coming from another planet, not really. And as we grow up, society starts working on us, conforming our minds, so that we too, can begin thinking like the million other robots that it has successfully created.

And soon there comes a time where, without our knowledge even, we're already conditioned, already confined in the shackles of stereotypes. And then there hardly seems a way out. If you continue living with those shackles, you sacrifice your happiness, and if you dare to break free of all boundaries, you stand the chance of being shunned.

As a woman, a young lady stepping into adulthood, I'm well able to feel my restrictions, these ropes holding me back. There's a constant pressure on me to dress a certain way, speak a certain way, and even eat in a certain manner. I may sacrifice my comfort but I must not go against society's rules, made especially for young ladies. And where did these rules come from, anyway? Didn't they just come from a bunch of narrow-minded people who cannot bear to lose control over a woman, and so, use their tiny minds to form rules which entrap a woman in even smaller cages, and ensure that their large empty vessel of an ego remains intact?

Why? Why is it so difficult for us to take the first step? To simply speak up?

If there's someone telling me to dress a particular way, why is it so difficult for me to tell them that ladies me who shall be wearing the dress, and therefore, my comfort is more important than their choice.

Why is it so difficult to open our mouths, so we can shut the wide mouths of those tiny-minded creatures?

As a woman, I am not obligated to comb my hair when I go to the supermarket, or wear something glamorous when

I go to a party. I am not obligated to wear a dress and high heels when I go to a disco, or wear a shirt long enough to cover my stomach. I am not obligated to put on make-up to cover my pimples, or freckles, or dark circles. I am not obligated to look pretty for any man or any woman either, for that matter. If I want to wear my pajamas to a party, or skip the makeup and heels, it is my choice. It is my choice- to do what I want, when I want, and however I want to.

Pretty is not the rent that I pay to exist as a woman in this world.

It is my choice entirely. Whether I dress up to please myself, or 'dress down' to be comfortable. It is my choice entirely whether I eat noodles with a fork instead of a pair of chopsticks at a Chinese restaurant or not. It is my choice whether I wish to speak in a loud voice or not, whether I say something harshly true, and downright rude, or not. You do not have the right to judge. Nobody does. You do not have the right to judge my character on the basis of the length of my dress, or decide my nature on the basis of the kind of spectacles I wear. It is not my hair length, clothes' length, my spectacles, or the amount of make-up I put that decides who I am.

It is the kind of books I read, the kind of dreams I dream, the kind of bonds I form with people. That is who I really am.

What do you think beauty is all about, anyway? Is it about the skinny legs, the perfect teeth, the tanned skin, or the perfectly applied make-up? No, I'm sorry, but that's called being pretty. But that won't last forever.

Prettiness is known to fade with youth.

What stays, however, is beauty. Inner beauty that tends to show on the outside, too, and lasts forever.

Beauty, real beauty, is the scar on your knee that you got from a scuffle with your brother, the 12year-old you with braces, as you chase a cute little puppy you've fallen in love with. Beauty is the make-up that melts in a cold shower after a hot humid day. It is the dry skin you get from relaxing in the pool too much. Beauty is the way you babble after a few too many drinks, the way you take off your heels an hour after you stepped into the party, so that you can dance the night away. Beauty is the way you dance in the rain, despite knowing you'll catch a cold the next day. Beauty is the way you choose hamburgers and fries over steak and champagne. Beauty is the loud laugh of a joke only you understand; it is the tears that sappy romances bring to your eyes. Beauty is when you let yourself free of all shackles, when society's opinions no longer matter to you. That kind of freedom is true beauty. Beauty is when you raise above all petty fights, insecurities, and realizes that you're at your best when you're being yourself and those who don't love you for who you are, don't really deserve you. Beauty is when you no longer need someone to constantly remind you to love yourself or care for yourself.

That kind of beauty, that kind of belief in yourself? It's dangerous.

That no negative thought, no negative energy can destroy you, let alone touch you, it's a different level of beauty. To know that only you hold the power to let things affect you, it's a dangerous revelation. And if used wrongly, it alone is enough to destroy you, to leave you devastated. So it's important that you use this power you hold over yourself wisely. And it is equally important that you love yourself, love the beauty of messy hair and tired eyes.

It is important that you learn to love yourself, because if you yourself won't, then who will?

Beauty is much, much more than skin deep and when you finally realize this, acknowledge it, accept it, that beauty inside you is bound to show on the outside. The glowing eyes, the vibrant aura around you, it's your inner beauty shining through. So don't shun it, don't destroy it with your over thinking, with negativity in any form.

Embrace it.
Embrace the beauty in you, and more importantly,
embrace the 'you' in you.
After all, beauty is at its peak when you're being yourself.
So don't hold yourself back.
Be yourself, love yourself.
The world will fall for you too.

CHAPTER TWO

LIFE

Have you at any point truly paused for a minute or two and contemplated life?

If you have, you're one of many. Nobody realizes what genuinely occurs in the afterlife. So you need to figure out how to appreciate life while you have it. Life can be confounding some of the time. However, you need to figure out how to simply go with it. Some time or another all that will bode well. However, up to that point, giggle at the disarray and grin through the tears.

Remember all that happens, happens for a reason.

What screws us up in life the most is the image that we fabricate in our minds of what it should be like. Everybody needs to try to forget that image in their mind. That image is the thing that society needs you to see.

Allow me to ask you a question. Furthermore, answer sincerely.

Would you be able to recollect who you were before the world revealed to you who to be? If you can't, you need to pause and take a look at everything in your life. You need to assess what lead you to turn into this individual.

What's more, assuming your answer is "it's what the world advised me to be" you need to advise yourself that this is your life, your story, your book. You don't have to let any other individual compose it for you. You don't have to apologize for the changes you make.

Consider life an excursion.

The best part isn't showing up at your destination; it's all the wild stuff that occurs in the middle. You need to fill your existence with memories, not materialistic possessions. Have stuff to tell, not show. You need to live for the minutes you can't articulate.

And, remember nothing grows without rain. So learn to embrace the storms of your life because they help you to grow.

A few people believe that life is finding somebody you need to go through it with. Yet, it's far beyond that. Like going on experiences, and meeting new companions. Or on the other hand, wandering around the city around evening time and writing on bathroom stalls.

Do everything with love; however, don't romanticize life like you can't survive without it.

Work on being in love with the individual in the mirror who has experienced so a lot but is still standing strong. Figure out how to adore the sound of feet while leaving something that was not implied for you. Be dauntless chasing what sets your spirit ablaze. Search for something positive every day, regardless of whether you need to look somewhat harder.

Live for yourself and be cheerful all alone. It isn't any less lovely. I guarantee.

Maybe the journey isn't much about becoming anything. Maybe it's about unbecoming everything that isn't you.

Discover your passion throughout everyday life. For example, mine is dancing. For me, dancing resembles a medication. It takes the entirety of my feelings, dread, outrage, nervousness, and washes them away. Your energy is the way to appreciate life.

Also, the fact that your way is distinctive doesn't mean you're lost. Also, remember, the very bubbling water that softens the potato, solidifies the egg.

It's what you're made of that matters, not the conditions. By the day's end, you can focus on what's destroying you or what's keeping you together. And when you figure out, pause and glance around, because this life is pretty amazing.

CHAPTER THREE

To Be Perfect

I've had a fairly significant morning by leaving on an endeavor to understand *"perfection"*.

The possibility that perfection even exists in our vocabulary puzzles me. No individual is great and capable of perfection.

So why are there certain individuals on this planet whose very objective is to solid arm themselves and everybody around them to attain perfection (a somewhat mythical state if you were to ask me)?

Why can't we simply be happy with how we are, with our steady enhancements and our developments? What's the significance here to be great? I think for me a feeling of happiness and a feeling of mental harmony are undeniably more significant than the race to attain perfection.

I want to learn and improve personally however I truly don't see the purpose in battling and battling and leaving mind and debilitating my substantial energy to arrive at some state which till now has stayed unclear.

What is perfection?

What characteristics must one have to be considered as perfect?

Who decides these characteristics?

Are these characteristics exposed to the changing occasions or do they stay consistent all through time?

It's generally very abstract and exceptionally easily proven wrong.

Maybe perfection is utilized as a persuading device for individuals to continue improving and developing and turning out to be better people?

I can't say I concur with this altogether.

The requirement for perfection can likewise be dangerous to the human mind in making clashes between the thing is and what something should be in an individual's assessment, which may thus leave them feeling insecure about themselves for not having achieved what they think they have. This being said, some people can only be driven by such challenging quests as attempting to attain perfection.

I surmise the key untruths of human development. We as a whole need to develop as individuals for humanity's advancement. Furthermore, the best way to do such is through enhancements and innovative headways, and scholarly development.

Perfection has presumably been utilized in the past to rouse individuals to move and develop. However, I think it was utilized excessively for the most part for the entirety of mankind, thereby neglecting to account for the fact that different people are motivated in different ways. Similar inspiration strategies probably won't work for all individuals.

So if taking a stab at attaining perfection isn't your thing, utilize some other type of inspiration. The fact is to develop and continue progressing and not stagnating.

I can securely close my analysis on perfection (according to my viewpoint) by alluding to a statement I found online by Lauren King, which summarizes how I feel about the entire idea: **"There are two sorts of perfect: The one you can never accomplish, and the other, simply by being yourself."**

Nobody is perfect
Don't try to fit in
Just be you and wreck it
Cause time is running thin

CHAPTER FOUR

The Direction To Self Love

Sometimes we arrive at points in our lives where we start evaluating where we stand, where we were, and where we are going. Doing this improves our sense of purpose, by giving us some guidance in our lives. This makes our lives more useful and valid.

Nonetheless, there are times when you simply don't have the foggiest idea where the road of life will take you. You can't make certain of things as they are or as they will be. Vulnerabilities will consistently be there. In some cases, things will not turn out well for you, regardless of how much heading and center your arrangements and acts have.

In those times, when things appear to be going appallingly out of track you had envisaged, you need to hold your confidence that things will take a turn for the great.

You may think you are lost, which might be true. However, being lost isn't always an awful thing. In some cases you find another perspective or side of yourself. This period of disclosure is often the best and most required. I suppose it is on the grounds that during this stage, what happens is your actual self comes out. Your actual self goes ahead and comes to articulation since it has arrived at a point where it is as of now not reluctant to be seen.

This deficiency of hindrances and fears is probably the best thing that could happen to a person.

You get liberated.

Independence from the evil spirits in your mind and every one of the weaknesses in your heart.

This opportunity is so freeing and is extremely, helpful for you arriving at your actual potential. You can find a sense of contentment in yourself. Freedom from your own concerns and nerves and frailties.

Not all who are meandering are lost.

At times they are simply looking for their tragically missing selves. It is a journey of self disclosure. One that closures in self-esteem and self-acknowledgment.

CHAPTER FIVE

Hopes And Fears

There are So many feelings moving us.

Happiness, sadness, guilt, but there is no feeling as terrifying as fearing something.

At the point when we think about fears, we consider the most moronic things on earth: creepy crawlies, bugs, statures... In any case, there is one that is much more important than all of these combined: *THE FUTURE.*

Future is a serious issue to talk about. It's one of the few things that make our lungs run out of breathing by just thinking about it. Its uncertainty and the measure of potential outcomes encompassing it makes us insane. In addition, our minds tend to turn us to terrible situations rather than good ones, which is the reason we are so scared of the future.

Since we're young, our peers define a whole path for us. We go to school, a couple of years after we pick a particular area to study and in college, we graduate on something related to those areas.

We are down for that until we reach a crossroad and don't have the foggiest idea about which road to choose. We feel like "alright, I've done everything, what's next?" That is the hardest piece of this cycle.

What's in store for us?

That question is difficult to answer since we don't have a crystal ball to foresee what's to come. The truth is that people prepare us to continue having plans, completing secondary school, attend a university, and get a new line of work... What on the off chance if we don't?

This routine is sick because people constrain us to settle on immense choices when we're young. At 15 years old we need to choose which area we want to study, for instance.

Is it true that we are prepared for that responsibility?

Frankly, I don't think so.

At times we pick a subject and afterward things don't work out because we don't see ourselves doing that. It occurs and afterward, we change. Indeed individuals around us will say that we don't have a clue what we need.

Is it true that we should know at such young age? We are intended to be young to do certain things, however mature enough to consider our future?

That doesn't sound great to me. In any case, we pick what we feel suits us the most.

After secondary school, we choose to go or not to attend a university. Here is another issue. We may pick a decent graduation program; however, will it be the one? We'll never know.

This is the place where the future comes to play once more. You don't have the foggiest idea what will occur, however you stay on track. If it doesn't work, you can have a go at something different still not realizing what will occur. But you still try.

All things considered, college isn't the circumstance where the future comes messing around with your head. After college is the point at which it comes. The strain to get a new line of work, the vulnerability, everything gets you. It's difficult to deal with, yet in case you're sufficiently centered and separate your feelings of trepidation from reality, it will all come around.

We as a whole have expectations and dreams to get a decent line of work, but if we don't a few months later, we will consider we are bound to deal with what we think is "awful work". We lost years and years studying for nothing.

Let me tell you something: those weren't a waste of time. They were worth it. And if you do have to work on those places, do it. Everything will come around. Those experiences are amazing because you get to know different things in your life and learn more about yourself. You will gain other abilities that will become advantages in the near future.

The thing that you need is to keep going and fighting for your dreams. If you do, the future will be the least of your problems. You'll have faith and strength to carry on. Hopefully, you will have your Dream job; have whatever you want to in life. All it takes is little hope and a fearless mind. Everything will come eventually. And about the future?

Well, when you find what you love and fight for it, who cares about the future?

Believe in yourself and when the right time comes, you'll reach the top of the mountain.

CHAPTER SIX

Dark

I've always found some comfort in the dark.

It's spooky, mysterious but also brings out the deepest thoughts, feelings and truths.

Like a warm blanket, takes you on a journey. At first, your cold but as you adjust, it gets warmer, lighter, and cozier and then you'll find yourself better with than without it. It might break you apart but also placing you back where you belong. Take you on a roller-coaster but bringing you back up where you were supposed to be.

You find yourself after losing so many pieces while traveling around the globe. Those were meant to leave so that you could rebuild yourself with new challenges, new people and, more importantly, higher fences.

You're the most important person in your story.

Don't let others write it for you or simply taking away your power. Sometimes it's a hard task because people get into your business, then your heart and rip it. They are cannibals, feeding by a bath of blood, pieces taken as time goes and satisfied with our misery. And it actually might take years to heal the scars, get rid of that nasty way of living. The bleeding is too hard to stop, cuts are deeper and the wounds have been scratched for too long, but once you do... Wow, there is no better feeling in life. There was no nurse or doctor around; you were your own medicine.

This empowerment that comes from grieving over relationships transformed you. Your heart is not as heavy to carry and your mind is no longer a problem to deal with. You feel fresh as water, strong as a rock, light as a feather and relieved as the team who saved the match in the last minute of the game.

It's a new version, a glow up, a grown up person with a better understanding of live and its obnoxious equations. With new characters coming to play, hopefully bringing out the best of you, staying as the sea kisses the shore so effortless and when it hits the stones fiercely.

You know, there are people who are similar to stars. They look little in the sky, but if you get to know them and look closer, are bigger than a planet. Their shine might fade sometimes but it's still there. And they're special. Wherever you move, they will follow, if you look at them they will shine brighter just to reassure you that they are there for you, and they will guide you home when you feel like your heart got lost in the city.

Everyone deserves a chance. There is always something you can learn from them, experience and put your life in perspective with that.

One stop doesn't define the end of the road just because of the sign.

You can wait breath and move on. Don't let other people keeping you from getting the love that you deserve. Love and let others love you.

The road is long and there are obstacles everywhere you go. It's up to you to live restricted or accept that fact and embrace another fall, a sore knee, get up and move to another trip.

It might get dark again, but will be easier. Who walks through hell and back once, can easily do it again. You know the way, the stumbles, its tricks and how to get back again.

Take a deep breath and go, don't look back. You'll find comfort in your darkest moment and somehow make it through.

Feeling Lost

It's a unique something where you can be something without really being something. An illustration. Something that addresses a bigger picture.

As humans, we can "be lost" without actually being truly uncertain of our physical surroundings. Being lost is a term that means to be unsure of your purpose and direction in life.

We as a whole encounter it; it's a typical piece of human instinct. These inconsistent considerations, they happen when we feel uncertain or insecure in our situations throughout everyday life. The best way to traverse this is to take some time to consider your ethics and your journey.

Everybody has a day to day existence venture, a course that their life follows. For a few of us, the fatalistic ones, we feel that this is preresolved. We feel the stars have their own arrangement that converts into our predeterminations. Then, at that point there are those among us who don't feel that the universe has a set arrangement that our lives follow.

As is commonly said, "Each to their own."

However, it doesn't make any difference which side of the fence you sit on, for a way is as yet a way. With regards to this hypothesis, which will here on be named as "the life path," there are a few principles.

First of all, you are certainly the key factor in "the life path."

Everything you accomplish is a result of the means you have taken and the lengths you will take. Returning to our unique difficulty: when you can't see this way unmistakably things can get overpowering.

The best thing to do is to relax. Nothing closes well when one is animated.

Then, take the necessary steps to cause you to feel loose. A decent cup of tea is my go to type of relaxing. Then, turn to writing a list. Lists are incredible in the manner they put things into viewpoint. Scribble down the things you represent or things you have confidence in.

Basically, you are helping yourself to remember the ethics you hold. Then, at that point guarantee you know your objectives. You're not expected to have everything outlined, so even a basic objective, for example, being happy will suffice.

From that point, it is in your hands. Pay attention to your heart as it discloses to you how to accomplish your goals and stay on the right path.

In case you are still extraordinarily lost, looking for help is a brilliant thought. Somebody who understands you, will indeed want to assist. Most importantly, be patient and positive. Good things take time and to redeem the awards you need to understand this.

Additionally understand that everybody gets confounded now and again, you are definitely not the only person with regards to this. However as long you stay positive, remind yourself what is important, and be patient, things will fit properly.

CHAPTER EIGHT

Solitude

Have you at any point felt like you simply need to be left alone for some time?

Just left alone to your musings, so you can have a conversation with yourself, be without help from anyone else, just for a while?

A person who's actually very social, consistently around individuals, would want to be distant from everyone else more frequently than a thoughtful person who's, pretty much, in every case alone, by decision.

We as a whole need things we don't, or can't, have.

Often, I'll find myself surrounded by people, but, even as I stand in the heart of the crowd, I'd feel so alone, so lost, so empty. The people passing by would be just a blur, the cacophony of noises cease to exist and I can feel myself being pulled back, sucked into the void, even as I reach out to someone, anyone, to pull me back, snap me back to reality.

I understand that, throughout everyday life, there won't be anybody to be with me consistently. You'll have companions, yet you'll have nobody to impart your deepest sentiments and considerations to. It's time like these that show you the significance of self esteem and self-acknowledgment.

At the point when you're up at three in the evening, sobbing hysterically, you will have nobody to comfort you, aside from you. It'll be you who'll need to give yourself the solidarity to get a hold of yourself, stand upright, hold your head high, and say that you CAN do it, because you believe in yourself, regardless of whether another person does or doesn't.

There are times when there's so much going on in your mind, and you'd prefer to say it for all to hear, however there's nobody to tune in, to comprehend. At the point when you can't understand what's happening in your life, can't fold your head over changes occurring excessively quick, don't have the foggiest idea how you will manage your life, how you will begin or end something, that is the point at which you want to get away.

Escape from this world, from this pressure, from the steady pressing factor of being a sure way to find a way into society. At times like these, you're entitled to escape. It's justified. Everyone needs a fantasy they can slip into, only for some time, since it's their asylum, their place to think or let go.

Escape is fine as long as it's for a short time. Stretching it too much would mean that you're not temporarily running away from the stress, you're permanently running away from responsibilities and from duties. That is the point at which you become a coward, a weakling, an individual with no spine, with no boldness, without even an ounce of self esteem.

There's always a difference between loneliness and 'me' time. The biggest being that one is by choice and the other isn't.

You escape from this world to invest some energy with yourself, by decision. And you find yourself alone in this world, with no one to talk to or share your feelings with, definitely not by choice.

However, some place, ambiguously, you've settled on a decision as well. A decision to pull yourself down, not trust in yourself, to permit yourself to be second rate when contrasted with others.

Figuring out how to cherish isolation is simply the greatest thing you can accomplish for yourself.

For what reason would you adore yourself any less? For you can't do what another person can do? Have you at any point wondered, however, at any point addressed, regardless of whether that another person can do what you can? Don't go looking for pity. All you will get is heaps of criticism and ignorance. It's a harsh world where most people don't care about what you want, or how you're suffering.

But just because it's a hard world, doesn't mean you Stop loving or become heartless.

Everybody is entitled to their share of heartbreak, Falling in love, falling out of it. And think of it this Way. Every time your heart breaks, you're one Heartbreak closer to finding your one true love, your Destiny.

I know that it's difficult to be optimistic when the life you've built so carefully, so painstakingly falls apart right in front of your eyes and you're helpless to do anything but keep looking on, desperately.

In any case, you need to realize that on if you flounder in self-centeredness, attempt to suffocate in your tears; no one will come plunging down to be your guardian angel. Ultimately, it'll be you, and just you, and your choice to quit abiding your life.

But, let tell you something.

It's OK to break down. It's alright to cry, to punch, and to break things. It's alright to let out the entirety of your feelings, to release everything. It doesn't make you weak; it doesn't make you a defeatist. It makes you human. Also, being human is a great deal more significant than being perfect.

Since perfection is only a perception.

CHAPTER NINE

The Mind

There is no doubt that we all know what it's like when our minds takes over and allows thoughts to pop in our minds.

Our minds are our closest companions and most noteworthy foes at the same time.

The manner in which you look at the world is the doing of your mind; all that you see is a mirror reflection of the interpretations that happen up in the mind. The bunch of times your brain attempts to drive away your regular impulses can go undetected. However more difficult than one might expect, the key is to control within.

Your mind accepts numerous obligations. It's liable for those musings that lessen your certainty and misuse your self-esteem. It likewise takes control for the pressure and stress. There are a couple of determined changes you can make to attempt to single out the things that are worth fretting over.

1) Every day rituals - Each day incorporate a range of things that fulfill you. Your "happy place" can be accomplished through yoga, Netflix, or anything in the between. Consider what makes your everyday routine worth experiencing or more pleasant, and assign time for these things. This will help you assume responsibility for your feelings by fitting explicit exercises that you know without a doubt will make you content.

2) Pursue something that inspires you– If you discover motivation throughout everyday life, you will have something to turn to when that pesky mind misbehaves. This can be an individual that you gaze upward to or a field of study that opens your eyes. Being enlivened keeps on rousing you, and inspiration is the way to progress.

3) Remember that you are not your thoughts – The truth is the inner workings of you organs are multiple times more intricate than the process of thinking. However, you don't fixate on how your liver or kidneys work. With your thoughts you regularly say, "I'm," giving them a feeling of embodiment. You may think something; however you are not that thing. You need to recollect that your thoughts aren't really who you are similarly that influenza doesn't characterize you.

4) Speak out- If something pesters you to the point that is turns into a fixation, standing up is maybe the best thing to do. You can address anybody you please as it is the way toward gathering your contemplations that matters. Normally when you express your sentiments or considerations, you get a clearer viewpoint in your own head. Life Is never just about as terrible as it appears.

5) Sleep on it - This may appear to be conflicting to the individuals who contend that going to sleep unhappy is detrimental, but acting on impulse is a lot worse. Seemingly the most noticeably terrible thing on the planet may appear to be unique whenever you've had the opportunity to unwind and recover. It's an issue of shunning fixating so you can get the entire image of your concern instead of this tiny view.

6) Music - I have referenced this beforehand, that is simply because I completely embrace it as a relaxation technique. Music makes us feel. Words that reverberate through a resonant voice can be more moving than understanding words. If you haven't got a playlist that gives solace, make one as quickly as time permits.

CHAPTER TEN

The Fighter

A lonely road,
An empty heart
A heavy mind
That same old mode.
The car was cold
Her skin was dry
The tears tickled her eyes
But had fallen so much
That now there were no tears left to cry.
She hit hard on the ground,
The fall was short,
but the impact was too painful.
Result of high hopes and expectations for a wild love,
for a new angel.
But as the sun came up,
As the darkness turned into light,
She put on her armor
And faced her fight with a smile.
Her soul was tired,
Her heart was jaded
But the flame inside her was far from being faded.
Despite all the odds she stood from the crowd,
Raised her hand in victory.

Lost so many battles but won a war,
A fight between herself and the curse
That they had given her.
She still struggles to breath,
She is still looking for that special feeling,
But we all know what is underneath,
A little fighter with big dreams.
Don't keep her inside,
Set her free and let her run towards the light,
Let her flame burn it all down,
Because there are so many things
Out there to be found.
One day she will be reminded as
The fighter without a weapon,
She didn't need a sharp knife or a big gun,
All she ever needed was her soul,
That wild spirit and beautiful heart
who would hold the world.

CHAPTER ELEVEN

Self-Believe

Self-believe is important, however, being fair with yourself is equally important. The harder you are on yourself, the likelier you are to break yourself.

There is a fine, barely recognizable difference between self-development and destruction, and while you think that analyzing every single mistake benefits you, it may well be harming you.

Constant negativity, when coming from an inborn source, is the absolute worst kind. Ambition and drive are keys to any type of success; however, driving yourself to fatigue will subvert all your persistent effort.

If you need to take a break, don't feel guilty – you are entitled to do things you truly appreciate, offering yourself a reprieve from the undertakings you don't discover pleasurable. Life is a journey and regardless of whether you haven't accomplished all that you set off to, you're still a better-developed individual than you were last week.

Strength comes from experience both good and bad. There is a difference between hard work and taking on an excessive amount to deal with. Part of success is being able to identify when this scale tips against you and taking steps to distress.

It takes a tough individual to venture from a destructive circumstance. Harping on your errors takes energy and is undermining. Challenge the negativity and focus on moving forward. Errors are unavoidable; however, how you manage them is particularly in your hands.

Rather than picking situations apart, take what went wrong and let it serve as a lesson. When moving forward, attempt to keep things in context. Ask yourself if something is as bad as it seems and think about what you can do differently in the future.

There are countless difficulties throughout everyday life so don't let your thoughts be another one. You should be your best friend and not your worst enemy.

In a world loaded with variables, your contemplations and mentalities are constants; you will consistently have them with you.

Given that, figure out how to cherish yourself as a blemished individual and permit yourself to commit errors. Understand that taking time out to collect your thoughts is completely finefrequently suggested. In a world where you'll always have yourself, there is no reason to feel guilty for doing what you need to keep a healthy and positive mindset.

I may not know you personally, but I just want to congratulate you on all you have achieved up to this point and remind you not to be so hard on yourself.

CHAPTER TWELVE

Reassurance

At the point when we are searching for a significant other to spend the rest of our lives with we're not just searching for a perfect partner.

We look for a warm embrace, glue that will pick up the pieces and put them back together, a generator that will keep the lights on when they don't have the strength to light up the dark.

In particular than the entirety of this, we search for strings. Somebody who will not give up regardless of whether his/her life is in question to save you. Somebody straightforward and legit as water who won't ever mislead you and will wash away every one of the negative considerations.

We search for some consolation, an uncommon condition in a conventional world.

There are a couple of individuals who stay in silence when you weep . They shut down their thoughts and turn on their ears for you. Some silences speak louder than words. When everything is falling Around you, the ice is breaking and all that there is left is a shell of the iceberg, they will make sure that the tiny piece won't break. They will take advantage of the water and take you to the shore, making you stronger.

They will have a blanket and wrap it over you, ensuring that you don't become sick and be more worse than you already are.

While their arms are around you, you'll gradually feeling good, warmer, and prepared to talk further about it and pay attention to their feelings. That is consolation.

At the point when you're on the edge of falling, they will get your hand and pull you up.

At the point when you're eager for advices they will not stop for a second in feed you with their benevolence, support and smart words. That is reassurance.

In case you're stuck in a corner and neglect to get out, they will come and protect you. That is reassurance .

All those actions, words and gestures are equal to reassurance. It's simple math.

They will be there, ensuring you're dressing appropriately for the climate, dealing with you when you're sick and ensuring you're taking care of yourself physically and mentally.

Furthermore, regardless of whether they're a great many miles away, they will be there.

One call, one message away, one basic sign and they will be there for you, ready to give you that live, assist you with discovering the passion that you lost and reassuring you that no matter what, you'll always have a companion.

CHAPTER THIRTEEN

Acceptance

All of us humans
Have our own little insecurities.
It leads us from hiding
Or even changing our identities.
It can be the reason
Why you're changing yourself,
Or the reason why
You're trying to be someone else.
But bear this in my mind
You're already beautiful.
Bear in mind,
You are amazing and wonderful.
Stop belittling yourself
And get off that brink.
You're already loved,
More than what you think.

When you arrive at this point in your life where nothing much matters, there are a few translations of this perspective. There are the individuals who might say you've gotten bored. Others would say you have lost the feeling of direction that once directed your contemplations and activities. Some may even say you have "copped it" or "given up". A couple may proffer the idea that it's simply a phase...... a period of what?

By one way or another, when you have experienced such a huge amount in your life, I trust it solidifies you, not to where you can't feel anything by any stretch of the imagination, yet to where your edge of feeling things - fortunate or unfortunate - is a lot higher than every other person.

For instance, you probably won't get as amped up for things as others or you may simply be in a never-ending condition of fervor since you know the worth of that bliss in a world like our own.

Or on the other hand you may be consistently careful and things will not hit you as hard as they did, because by then you have seen everything. Nothing truly stresses you, when you contrast it with the bigger plan of things.

I feel this "stage" is the best. It implies you have adequately developed to realize how to acknowledge things.

It implies you have figured out how to adjust your whimsical, utopian Disney land thoughts with a weighty portion of the real world and the facts of life.

It implies you can be cheerful and miserable without letting either feeling influence your emotional equilibrium.

It implies you have one consistent perspective that can't be influenced by the glimmers of feelings, while having the option to feel things like every other individual.

It's a decent "stage" where you figure out how to be more tolerating of the status quo around you.

For what reason is this acceptance so significant?

It is SO VERY significant. It is so inseparably connected to your mental soundness and true serenity that without acknowledgment, your mind will continually be in a condition of fit.

Your brain will append the happenings of the world to your self - regard and your sentiments and your point of view, and afterward an endless loop will begin.

It is the circle that drives you to always failing to be content. Satisfaction and inward wellsprings of joy are the best way to navigate the road of life.

Analysts would call this "locus of personality" expressing that it could either be external to us (where we see ourselves as others see us) or inner (where we see ourselves simply as per our instinct).

I like the later decision. Furthermore, the best way to get to that second kind of having an inward locus of personality is acknowledge things that are in your control, and the things that are not in our control. A quiet acknowledgment of life's numerous impulses and changes and highs and lows, is the best way to live calmly, and joyfully.

You can't make a huge difference. Also, as a rule you can't transform anything, however yourself.

So change yourself to be more accepting and more understanding that you are your solitary way to "endure" and "exist" or to "live".

The decision is with you. Acceptance is the most ideal approach to settle on the decision.

CHAPTER FOURTEEN

Memories

The arrangement of memories having a place with the gigantic library of our mind continues to develop.

Consistently, new parts are created in the city and the term of every one is to some degree short.

At times, the timetables keep us from broadening them for quite a long time, despite the fact that time requests that it ought to be enjoyed as if it was the last block of chocolate on the tablet.

In any case, the primary individual answerable for not exploiting time is the person, who doesn't comprehend that tomorrow is a hallucination and the present is important for the real world.

You can't reason correctly when these two fleeting universes impact.

In your mind, tomorrow is not far off and, therefore, you can enter the stage again to play another scene in your life with the same character. This perspective on the realities appears to be right; but the person can leave, leaving you with the void of disappointment.

This feeling is destructive, in spite of having no evident importance. In case it was impractical to impart the phase of life to the same character voluntarily, then, at that point it appeared to be the most right at that point.

More to this, attitude values the relationship established with the other person, since the need to remain close to them and to reinvent the recipe for their friendship is visible, strengthening and perfecting it.

There are always edges to be filled and new treasures to be discovered, which must be kept and preserved again, not in a museum showcase in plain sight, but in ours in the museum of trust.

Gathering antiquities of this nature and shielding them from the external makes us raise our worth with others and become enormous, paying little heed to the properties that have a place with us, since individuals resemble gold: when they are true, they have a high esteem and trust us, without having to know the measure of progress that lives in our pocket

Once bogus, they seek to know what is our own to acquire profits by it. The former will remain perpetually in our memory gathered in the comedy or romance section, while the others in the horror section.

We all want to be a part of novel brimming with love and joy, however for that it is important to be reasonable and cautious while we're writing the narrative , since we're the ones in particular who can shift its direction and carry it to an effective end.

CHAPTER FIFTEEN

Braver Than You Believe

Have you ever been the pillar of strength for someone?

The one people always lean on; always count on, to support them. The one who's been strong for so long that the idea of weakness, the very concept of being vulnerable to something seems foreign.

Have you ever experienced being the bigger person always?

The one, who sacrifices, compromises, moulds her according to the likes and dislikes of people she loves, so that their comfort isn't affected?

Have you ever wondered what a confidant feels, what their emotions are?

They're forever storing secrets deep in their heart, carrying the burden of responsibly keeping them safe.

But what about their secrets? Ever wondered who they share it with?

A person can give, and give so much to people he loves, but there's only so much he can give to others and give up for them.

There comes a time when you've given so much that there's nothing left to give and you're left with an empty feeling in your heart and a blanket of loneliness trying to smother you.

Wouldn't things have been different if you'd given and taken? Maintained a balance? At least, it wouldn't have led you to lose yourself completely, right?

How long can you be strong?

How long can you ignore your own problems in your quest to solve those of others?

Don't you have the right to simply let go, relax, and take a breather, live for yourself, for once?

Don't you have the right to chase your dreams too?

To make mistakes, learn from them, gather experience, go out into the world, explore and fulfill your desires?

How long can you keep up this mask of optimism?

How long can you constantly cover up your fears, your pain?

It isn't like you don't have fears, you don't feel pain. As a matter of fact, for you, it's ten times worse.

To silently bear the pain, hide it behind a smile, is the most difficult thing anybody can do.

How long are you going to strain a smile, will it to reach your eyes, even as you cry yourself to sleep every night, silent sobs wracking your body?

There's a limit to everything. There's only so much pain you can bear, only so much of a smile you can strain. And when that limit's been crossed, you snap.

You break down, fall apart. And there's nothing and no one to stop you.

Just like there's nothing and no one by your side as you crumble down.

The wall you'd built around your heart, to protect it, is broken, all at once. The emotions you'd managed to keep at bay, crash over you, leaving you bewildered, as you struggle to breathe, to live, even as these emotions keep pulling you under.

And that is why you learn to swim. Swim through these swirling emotions, trying to make head or tail of these changes taking place around you, trying to break free.

You're alone in this battle, though. People will sympathize, yes. But there'll be very few who'll empathize. You'll have to fight your demons, ward off the evil threatening your very existence.

You'll have to pull together all the broken pieces of you, make yourself whole again. And you'll have to do it on your own.

Nobody can do that for you, nobody. Not the person you love the most or the person who means the most to you.

Only you know your heart, and yourself.

And remember, it's okay to have weaknesses. But what isn't okay is allowing people, or even yourself, to use those weaknesses against you.

Make your weaknesses your strength. Even if you can't, love your weaknesses as much as you love your strengths. They won't be much of weaknesses if you love them wholeheartedly, accept them completely.

Sometimes, being too strong can become a weakness. Sometimes, people can use this against you.

Why be a pillar that can be broken with one blow of the hammer?

If you want to be strong, need to be, for the people you love, be the base, the very foundation. Nothing, no blow, no disaster, no calamity can break it. It always, always stays put. Not many people understand its importance, but without it, nothing can survive, nothing can stand.

Don't be the color that blends into the background, that nobody notices or values.

Be the color that stands out, stands tall, even among a hundred others.

Be strong because you want to. Be weak if that's what you want. But don't be something that you don't want to be, or that isn't you.

Be the real you, and before anyone else falls for you, you'll end up falling for yourself.

Do things. Go for it. Whether good or bad, it'll be an experience you'll cherish when you're too old, too crippled to do anything but reminisce.

Love life the way it is. It could have been so much worse, or so much better. But it wouldn't have been something that you love.

Because no matter how your life is, remember, it's what you've built yourself, with all your hard work and choices you made.

Love life, quietly, loudly, however you want. But love it, and you'll be the happiest person on earth, in your own unique way.

Love life with all of you. Love life till it consumes you.

It'll be worth it. I promise.

CHAPTER SIXTEEN

Nothing Is Permanent

Some time ago, if people would've told me that nothing's permanent in life, I would've looked at my mother and wouldn't have bothered to remember what they said.

But it's only when certain things happen to you, that you realize that nothing is permanent in life. Everything, everybody eventually goes away. It moves away from you, or moves on. Feelings, emotions, materialistic possessions, people, you name it, and it's all temporary. Nothing is a permanent fixture in our life. This is why it's important to find happiness within yourself and the nature that surrounds you.

Even your emotions aren't permanent. So learn to love yourself, for who you are.

Don't let people's actions, people as a whole, affect you. Learn to get rid of them, especially those whose only job is to bring you down. However good some people may be to you, don't forget, they're only going to be there for so long.

They can give you a fleeting sense of happiness, but if you're looking for permanent happiness, start looking for it in yourself.

Nobody gives you enough importance, because, believe me, there are very few people out there for whom you are of ultimate importance. There are very few for whom you are the first priority. Your parents are among those few, to begin with. But for friends, for people you love, who don't love you back, there's very few for whom you'll be of unparalleled importance.

This is exactly why self-love is so important. There'll come a time, eventually, when you'll have no one but yourself to hold onto, to comfort you, when everything is crumbling down.

But many a times, there's a conflict between my emotions, my feelings, my desires.

Sometimes, when people advice you to not cross oceans for those who don't even jump puddles for you, I disagree. I say, do it.

Cross oceans, Move Mountains, do it. Love openly, love wholly, love completely.

Fall in love without any harness, and if you get hurt, so be it.

Love with all you have, fall with all you can.

Be hurt. If nothing else, it will surely leave you a tad bit wiser. But whatever you do, give it all you have. Don't hold yourself back. Don't restrict yourself. Don't apply Terms and conditions to whatever you do. After all, you won't get another chance just like this one. So while you have the opportunity in front of you, grab onto it, and don't let it go. Use it. For all you know, it may never come back. Life and love isn't about what you gain, it's about what you give.

But, then again, keep in mind who you're doing this for.

Make sure that the person you're doing it for is worth it. Don't do it for a person who you love with all you have, but who refuses to recognize it, acknowledge it, treasure it, who refuses to reciprocate it. Don't do it for someone whose words hurt you, whose actions leave you devastated. Don't do it for someone who could care less about your well-being, your happiness.

They're not worth it and you don't deserve this.

You didn't sign up for this. This constant hurting, constant over-thinking, constant depressive thoughts. You've done nothing to earn these self-destructive thoughts.

Don't ever settle for less than what you deserve.

If you don't deserve certain people in your life, then you won't have them. It's a simple truth.

And, just like that, life can give you some good stuff to cherish too.

Maybe the good stuff comes in a badly wrapped package, or is hidden in a horribly cooked dish, but it's there. It is rights there, waiting for you to see it, grab it, and learn from it.

Life isn't all that bad. Sometimes, it gives you exactly what you need, even if it isn't what you want. Take it, however it comes because, at the end of it, you'll be a better person. You'll be a happier version of 'you'.

Sometimes, it may so happen that there are people you love too much for your own good. You can't imagine life without them; you can't imagine surviving without them. But if life believes that they're not good for you now, or in the long run, then that's the final verdict.

They're going to be gently pushed out, roughly shoved, or simply kicked out of your life.

But they will go away. Because that's what's meant to be. And that's exactly what will happen. Everything happens for a reason, everything is meant to be.

Choosing what color dress to wear, and your mood as a result, choosing what you want to become, choosing which college to go to, whom to become friends with, whom to fall in love with, it's all planned. Life already knows what will happen, and it plays you along

And here's the catch. There's nothing you can do to change it. Because there's no way to stop Destiny from doing its job, there's no way to stop it from changing lives.

Since Life will throw everything at your face anyway, you might as well be ready. And here's what you can do.

Stop regretting what's already gone and stop worrying about what is to come. Take one day at a time, because you don't know what destiny plans to do with you tomorrow. So live for today. Live in the present. Enjoy what is instead of worrying over what was and what will be.

Live for yourself. You are important. You are worth it.

Others see in you, what you'll never see in yourself. You're beautiful. You mean the world to someone somewhere. Remember that.

So when you'll walk away, remember that there will be someone who's going to miss you, long for you, regret losing you, but never stop loving you.

Why? Because you're worth it.

And then there's never a bigger revelation than knowing that you're being treated the way you deserve to be, that you're treating yourself the way you deserve to be.

Because you're beautiful, you're different, you're unique. You may not be perfect in the world's eyes, or even in the eyes of those who matter to you. But you're perfect for yourself. And that is more than enough.

Love yourself. Forget the world. Forget whether they love you or not.

As long as you love yourself, as long as you're content with yourself, as long as you're at peace with yourself, there's nothing and no one that can affect you, hurt you, change you. There's nothing negative that can touch you, if only you believe in yourself.

Be yourself. It's the greatest gift to give yourself.
Because remember, you are worth it. You do matter. Period.

CHAPTER SEVENTEEN

Art

Everything in life is an art. I mean everything, the way you dress, the way you express, and even the way you feel.

Life comprises little minutes. Minutes that can be more modest than everything but make your life.

If you begin living for the smallest of reasons that is how you know you're truly living. The smell of downpour after a rainstorm. The chilly breeze of a quick-moving towards winter. The warmth of the oven while baking. These loads of little subtleties make up your existence without you knowing it. Also, when you begin taking a look at things. Truly looking. You'll begin living. Then you'll see how it is to be a human in this world loaded with people.

What if you don't start living you?

Well. Consider the possibility that you wake up one day when you are 65 or 80 after chasing money and neglecting the seemingly little things. Consider the possibility that you wake up when you're 90 and recall that you didn't swim at the seashore or in pools because your thighs were wiggled. It will make you extremely upset. I'm not here to reveal to you how to carry on with your life. But I will say this. You must quit being so difficult on yourself. You're young and will figure it out on schedule.

I need you to pause and unwind briefly.

That load of considerations stressing you and all the worry just put it out of your mind for the moment. Now realize how beautiful it is to have lungs that permit you to breathe air. How astonishing and great it is to have legs that permit you to ascend mountains. It's a disgrace how at some point we underestimate them.

Presently how would you feel when I remind you that there are individuals who don't have legs? And, individuals who must have an oxygen tank to breathe. Presently how terrible do you feel? What about those individuals that have been underestimated like you've taken these straightforward things like breathing and legs for conceded?

Envision. An entire human being that has been underestimated. How would you imagine that feels? Some of you might even not need to envision. So that is the reason I emphasize this next point unequivocally. Continuously be the best individual you can be.

Be benevolent, in any event, when you're worn out. Be seeing, in any event, when you're furious.

Listen when somebody talks, truly tune in and quit considering how you will answer.

Make a special effort to show individuals you love them.

Be the best individual you can be and when you do something wrong, then, at that point compensate for it the following day, or moment, or second.

Also, never invest a snapshot of your energy attempting to demonstrate to somebody how incredible you are. Your activities will demonstrate that for you. Allow me to impart something individual to you in alright case.

I like a lot of things. For example, I like firecrackers. I like creatures. I like strawberries.

In any case, you know what I love?

I love the sensation of being alive.

You know the inclination you get not long before a major drop on a rollercoaster.

That sensation of adrenaline and dread. The sensation of knowing you're protected. Yet at the same time cherishing that sensation of falling.

I love the inclination you get when you're remaining in the downpour. Large sprinkles all over and wind in your hair. I like the sensation of being alive. The sensation of sentiments.

Presently do you get it?

Life isn't simply wonderful and delightful and wondrous.

Life is an art.

❧❧❧

Sometimes life is same as a painting
It can be full of colors, monochromatic or it can be
blank too
Every painting has some or other meaning shrouded
inside it
Sometimes it's easy to guess what it's all about
But sometimes it takes hundreds of years just to figure
out a small thing
Every artist wants their painting to be eminent
Parallel we also want to become eminent
But every painting cannot have that stroke of luck in it
Painting is a collective effort of many things
Each and every thing from a brush to the color palate
Plays a very important role to make the canvas
breathtaking
But not every one's born painter
Every stroke of brush adds up to make something
beautiful

In the same way every second till our death
adds up to what we call wonderful life

CHAPTER EIGHTEEN

Social Media

As a teen myself, the assumptions and pressing factors of online media are all around natural. I realize what it resembles to post an image on Instagram and anticipate the preferences, restlessly trusting the all out creeps up. The sensation of changing your profile picture on Facebook and anticipating the remarks that in some way or another decide your worth resonates with me. I get it. You may be thinking, that is fine but how would we conquer these feelings? If I knew the appropriate response, I'd have a smash hit book out on racks and be a millionaire in my simple young years.

Honestly, I am still working on it. There are a couple of things that I do know to be sure, nonetheless.

Right off the bat, a number has no importance in addressing your self- worth. You can't contrast years of existence for certain digits. On the off chance that you coherently consider this briefly, you will get what I am attempting to communicate.

How could a number recount a story that has been going on since the day you were conceived?

The second point I need to make is somewhat harsher, however rings just as obvious.

At the point when you add a photograph to any online media outlet, the quantity of individuals that glance at that image and truly care isn't so high. Your actual loved ones will take a genuine interest, yet a ton of your adherents will look through it, maybe twofold tap, however won't see it with any importance.

On the off chance that you don't trust me, take a look at it : if the photographs you posted were printed out and you could show them to anybody you satisfied, the greater part of your "supporters" could never make the rundown. Why? Since you understand they wouldn't mind enough to see the value in the messages behind the flicks. The equivalent applies to the online reality around us.

The last point I can make right presently is to never fail to focus on what is genuine. The things you see online are not destined to be genuine, yet the things you see outside and individuals you cooperate with eye to eye, they generally are.

We as a general public are failing to focus on ordinary magnificence; the charm of nature, the shrewdness of verbally expressed words and the enchantment of our instinctual capacities to peruse looks are nearly lost to us. Try not to misunderstand me in reasoning I detest online media, for I comprehend the advantages. My issue is the point at which it devours us and detracts from the worth of straightforward life. You are excellent all around because you are a piece of the idea of presence. We live on Earth with a great many animal categories, contingent upon them for endurance. As people, we are just a little spec in a more noteworthy picture.

In the plan of things, those remarks and likes amount to nothing. The seemingly insignificant details, the substantial things, they mean the world.

My companions, we are on this planet for an explanation, and that reason is unquestionably not to discover a feeling of endorsement in numbers that come from individuals we don't genuinely have the foggiest idea. Try not to permit yourself to be disappointed by the domains of web-based media and let it assume control over how you feel about yourself. Simply existing in itself is something holy that has such countless layers of intricacy that make it a fearless accomplishment.

Life is amazing, so if you are living it, so are you.

CHAPTER NINETEEN

Changes

You change so much over time without even realizing it. You're not a similar individual you were a year prior, a month prior, or even a day prior. Looking at this logically, it feels so normal to change. There's something so implicit about it. In any case, something unnervingly delightful about it as well.

Also, some of the time something comes into your life and changes everything without you knowing. Your fate is continually being changed.

Life is so tumultuous but there's something truly entrancing about the mayhem.

It upsets us yet in addition powers our hearts to thunder such that it leaves us feeling so glorious and longing for additional. Also, you figure out how to cherish the seemingly insignificant details.

Like 5 AM dawns and 5 PM dusks that change the sky to inconceivable tones and road trips and bicycle rides with music blasting in your ears and wind in your hair And windows down on silent back roads And blinds moving around the house due to the cool wind that makes itself your visitor.

Also, at last, you figure it out. You deserve it all. You deserve love and peace and magic and happiness moving in your eyes. You deserve the happiness that makes you cry until you're powerless on your knees.

However, there will be days where you simply will want need to give up. Because you believe that the changes in your life aren't good and you can't manage them.

However, don't let the possibility of progress alarm you. However, it will be terrifying from the outset. Making a major life change is in every case pretty startling. In any case, that is OK. The things that alarm you additionally assist you with growing as an individual. You need to quit stressing over what could turn out badly and think about every one of the things that could go right. You may lose who you were to a great extent but it will assist you with discovering what your true identity is. You will break from time to time but that is okay. What's messed up isn't constantly intended to be fixed. Maybe it's intended to be changed.

The secret of change is to focus on building the new, not fighting the old. Sometimes your life has to be shaken up and reworked to get you where you belong. Furthermore, it may require a year or a day, but what's intended to be will discover a way.

Just remember to be yourself. Try not to be another bloom that is picked for its excellence and left there to rot and die.

Be a pink star jewel, the most uncommon pearl on the planet.

Furthermore, after the entirety of this occurs, sit down and recollect what you've experienced. How far you've come. How much strength and mental fortitude and persistence you have learned and created. So I believe it's an ideal opportunity to begin another experience.

CHAPTER TWENTY

Explore. Dream. Discover

Have you ever gone on any vacation, any kind of holiday? As a tourist, you're very eager to see this and to see that. You know that you probably won't come back to this place and so you're eager to see as much of it as you can.

But how many of you can truthfully say that you've actually, genuinely enjoyed a particular destination?

You've been so eager to take pictures, share them on social media, click the scene on a camera, that you've never bothered to capture the moment in your memory.

Have you ever just stood in a particular spot, closed your eyes, felt the wind rushing past your face or the sweet sun warming up your skin? Ever just stood to listen to the birds' songs, the crunching of leaves beneath their feet, as people walk past, or the waves crashing against the shore? Have you ever simply felt a place, so much so that it moves your soul?

Probably not. I can truthfully admit that, at least, I haven't.

Maybe I've never had the chance, or maybe I never used one, even though it was right in front of my eyes. Maybe it's the fact that everywhere that I've traveled to so far has been mainstream. I've always taken the road traveled more often, followed trails already made by others. I've never tried to create a trail of my own.

I'm a wimp when it comes to taking risks. Maybe that's why I've never allowed my desire for simply letting my heart lead me where it wants to, to take over. But I want to go places. Not just too all the ones people have always been to. I want to carry a backpack with a few pieces of clothing, a journal, my passport and some money and simply go. I don't know where, how or when. I just know that I've got to go, to search for some solitude, to discover myself, and maybe to treat myself to a slice of heaven while I'm at it.

I want to stand at the edge of a cliff, look down with my breath lodged in my throat, to see the waves breaking on the rocks, and then, to jump. Jump straight into the deep sea, to go deep enough that I can see the magic of life underwater, and then to break free, gasping for air, even as I revel in the adrenaline rush of it.

I want to sit at the edge of an isolated building and watch the sunset without worrying about what I'm going to do the next day or where I'm going to stay for the night.

I want to sit in a pub, or a cafe, and observe people around me, to see what ticks them, to try and learn little secrets about them by their gestures, their actions.

I want to go to a farm, to live there and help with the morning chores and know what real hard work is like.

I want to lie down in a field surrounded by flowers, as I stare into the night sky, trying to form patterns with the stars.

I want to make sand castles at the beach and watch the waves sweep it away.

I want to dance in the rain to the music of thunder. I want the wind to make my hair fly, and to make the flowers dance.

I want to discover new things by mistake, instead of visiting places that every tourist does.

I want to taste all kinds of cuisines or go scuba diving, hiking, or anything else even remotely daredevil.

I want to make a new friend, who doesn't understand me or the language I speak.

I want the sun to bleach my hair and to make the freckles on my nose stand out.

I want to taste every kind of food I can, till my stomach is about to burst and my jeans no longer fit.

I want to jump off a plane with only my parachute on my back and scream till I'm nearly deaf.

I want to dance in a land where I can't speak the language but can only speak with my eyes.

I want to dance till my feet hurt and sing till my voice is sore.

I want to go to places where ghosts are believed to exist, to discover the undiscovered, explore the forbidden.

I want to go into forests and see animals I'd believed only exist in picture books.

I want to get into food fights, and crush grapes under my feet and find secrets in old forgotten palaces.

I want to run my hands along words carved into walls in ruins, and imagine the lives of people who lived there.

I want to go to battlegrounds and imagine the people who fought to save their country, their livelihood, their families, their honor, and wonder with awe about their brave deeds.

I want to lose myself and satiate my wanderlust.

I want to go to churches and sit on the pew, staring at the stained glass windows, wondering what ran through the artist's mind when he made it.

I want to fall in love over and over again. With myself, with nature, with life.

I want to live life on my own terms, live for myself. I want to experience what it feels like to really live. I want to be perfectly imperfect, be a misfit, and stand out where I should blend in.

I want to be different. Different enough to be noticed but not so much that I'm shunned. I want to be free, mentally, emotionally.

I don't want to attach myself to something so much that it becomes a burden, a baggage I have to carry everywhere I go.

Once a year, I want to go someplace I've never been before.

CHAPTER TWENTY-ONE

Darkness Has Its Own Light

Do you ever feel like drowning? As you try to reach the shore, the water pulls you back in and even if you fight it, your muscles will get tired and your strength will be gone.

That is how your mind works. When you are in a dark place, you fight it, but the negative thoughts turn in to a cloud bigger than any blue sky you might want to create.

Sometimes life gets tough and you paralyze. You just don't know what to do. As you try to find a way out, it only gets worse. Everything becomes a huge weight on your shoulders, even the smallest things in your daily basis. college, the pressure from your family, your friends disappointments, other people's opinions. Everything surrounding you suffocates you and you just go with that lethal flow.

Being in a dark place is hard. You doubt of yourself, believe that you aren't worth of so many things, walk away from your circle of people because you feel like you are toxic... And then you're alone. Well, at least you try to be.

But then there are incredible people that help you to lift that weight. Once they notice your lack of confidence and self-love, they will do everything to keep you safe from that storm. If you're inside a deep hole, they will get a rope to get you. They take you higher, always bringing the best of you under the most controversial circumstances. In these particular situations, their power is outstanding. They distract you from whatever is going on but also remember that you can share with them your fears and anxieties. Even if you know you can trust them, it's so nice to hear that.

All people want is reassurance.

Dark places are hard to fight but every dark has its own light.

CHAPTER TWENTY-TWO

Perspective

Perspective is a big word, not only for its number of letters but also for its complexity. You see, everything in life it's about how we see and judge things. A single drop can turn into an ocean if we make a big thing of it. The same goes for something we are afraid of. Facing it is the hardest part, but then we realize we gave too much meaning to something that has no harm.

This is how our mind works. It has a twisted system that takes us to the edge.

But here is the thing: we are so stuck on the obvious that we forget to see the bigger picture.

Can you imagine you amazing that would be? How many relationships would still be alive? How much our lives would improve because of that?

But again, our emotions take the best of us.

Feelings and thoughts are a bad mixture. Sometimes, we overthink about how people feel about us and we get hurt. Others, we are rational and don't think about how someone else will feel as the result of our actions. It's a complete circle in which we are stuck on.

Who doesn't get in trouble for mixing things? I don't need an answer, because it's a rhetorical question. It's clear as water. Everyone does.

Our emotions control us more than we control ourselves. They make us feel in a certain way about something or someone and they change our perspective. Sometimes, not directly but they still do. In a group of friends, we tend to follow their patterns and values. If one of the members has something against someone else, it's enough for you to misjudge that person. We forget that she/he is also a human being, with feelings. We forget our flaws and search deep for theirs. We don't measure our words and spill them not realizing the impact it will have in someone else's life. Again, we don't see the bigger picture.

Just because someone is different, has other values or acts in a way that we don't understand, doesn't mean that person is less than us.

Everyone is special in their own way.

Perfection is an utopy and its up to us to Face that reality. Maybe we don't think we are perfect, in fact, we judge ourselves more than any other person. But when we judge someone else, we put ourselves on a pedestal.

We are better, bigger, stronger.

Guess what? It's all fake.

Those flaws we see in other people can be ours as much as what we see as flaws can be gifts. There are so many gifted people out there who are judged. Still, they are absolutely amazing on what they do. Probably that's why people judge them, they don't have that characteristic that allows them to be effortlessly incredible.

Being different does not mean being less. It means that you are unique, you have something amazing to share with other people and you get to show them what you can do.

A Portuguese poet used to say that we are from the size of what we see and not from our height. Couldn't agree more.

We can have all the richness in the world, but if we are empty inside, what does it worth? Nothing buys a peaceful heart or happiness. Little things give us those feels. We don't have to feel the best person on earth to earn that. All we need is to respect the other and be kind, not judging, but understanding. Not letting go, but staying. Supporting, not walking away. More than that: look at them and see a heart, not a face, a body or anything else that might be seen as a flaw.

At the end of the day, all we need is to see the bigger picture.

CHAPTER TWENTY-THREE

Trust

Life is crazy. It's incredible how things change in a blink of an eye and the worst of all is that you can't predict it. You know that tomorrow the sun will rise, that you have to go to work or to college.

What about the rest?

Life is uncertain and it's not because of destiny or karma. Just like everything else in this world, life is made of people and those are the ones who make it uncertain. We never know who will stay or leave, in who to trust or not. To be honest, the only person we are certain about its ourselves.

Don't get me wrong, being alone hurts in this world but how do we know if our friends are real? If our family will stand by us every step of the way? We don't.

The only person who will never leave its you. The person who will help you to get up when you fall it's you. Also, the person who will make you feel confident, it's you. You see, trust is a delicate thing. I always heard that it takes years to build it and seconds to lose. It's hard to face it, but is true. You can do one thousand amazing things, but if you screw up once, you're done. Doesn't matter if you had the best intentions or were not on a good day.

People will judge you and probably leave. This is how toxic people are today. Of course that there are cases in which we are forced to leave, but if we think so highly of those people, how does one single mistake brings everything down?

I don't know. I'm still trying to find that answer.

People claim they're thankful, but are they really? I seriously doubt of that.

One of the things I've learned from this year is that you can give the world to someone, but sometimes they won't make the same effort to give it back to you. In fact, they won't care. At the end of the day, they know you're there. The question is, are they there for you?

Probably not.

That's why more than trusting someone else, you need to trust you. In fact, you already do, even without noticing it.

People are important, but you are the most important person in your life. It takes time to figure that out, but that will come to your senses in time. So when it comes to trust, the only person you actually need to trust is yourself. There will be doubts, high mountains to climb and deep holes to come out from, but when you believe, you will make it. Trust yourself and you will be okay. Way better than if you live basted on what other people say. You're a person, you're worth it, and you will make it. All it takes is self-confidence and believe in you.

CHAPTER TWENTY-FOUR

Key Moments

There are key moments in our lives. Our first steps, first words.

All those milestones are important and everyone expects us to have them. In fact, sometimes we are pushed to accomplish them. I would say that push someone to do something is a very messy thing to do, but what if it's not someone, but something? Life for example.

Sometimes, life demands us to go deep and swim in deep waters. Some people say that all it takes to walk into the unknown is a leap of faith. That's a valid point, and down the road we need that leap of faith. The only problem is when life pushes you to go deeper and deeper and then there is no way to go back. Pressure is on and there is only one option: keep swimming. Otherwise, you'll drown.

But there is another scenario: what if you still drown? You can go deeper, you can climb to get a better view, but what if that effort turns into your enemy?

Being committed to something is a brave decision and you need to swim against the motion to achieve big things. All the stress, every worry takes a little bit more of you until you're vulnerable and you have no idea what to do.

Will you play it safe and lose everything?

Will you keep pushing and trying to reach a better view?

Or will you just face the fact that it's too much and you can't?

I don't know if any of these options is correct but I do know this: it takes little time to be vulnerable, but it takes a lifetime to allow yourself to feel vulnerable.

We always have that idea that we need to be strong. We can't be whining, we can't cry, we can't be weak, etc. Well, we should do all of this.

Taking time to be vulnerable is also taking time to get to know yourself better and learn how to deal with challenges in our daily basis.

You'll find out more about you when you are vulnerable then when you're happy. Not because being happy doesn't change your perspective, because it does, but being upset brings the fighter inside of you. It allows you to go deep down and analyze things closely.

When you're happy everything is sunshine and paradise. When you're down, you learn to value things.

If you are going deep, watch if the air is not being pulled out of your lungs and you're gasping for air. It's important to take big steps and accept new challenges but it's more important to save your mental health.

Make sure you know exactly what you're doing when you're crossing the road.

Sometimes there is just no turning back. And if there is, it's s not that easy to find the way back to where you truly belong. And if you crossed that road and you just lost your way, remember that there was a reason behind your choice.

Beyond all the problems and anxiety, there is a goal.

Keep that in mind and search for it.

Sometimes it's not down that road, but if you turn to a different corner, things might actually work for you.

CHAPTER TWENTY-FIVE

2020

Sparks of hope lighted the dark January night and a new year was born. It was filled with hopes and dreams, promises and amazing perspectives but their fate, our fate was completely sealed.

2020 was supposed to be a gift. Another year to be thankful for and another beautiful journey alongside with the ones we love. But there was a witch watching us outside, crossed paths with us along the way, gave us 2020 like a poisoned apple and we tasted it. In fact, we just ate it, because if we had tasted it we could have been cautious and enjoyed our time before much better. And then, the madness started. Mankind has felt freedom ever since we can remember, and now was trapped inside a bubble that could pop at any point, cause damage without hurting from the get go and silently deliver a death certificate within the following days, even hours.

In carnival, we wear masks because it's fun, but at some point we need to let go of them.

2020 brought a permanent mask, but left out all the fun, the no judgment feeling and the happiness we once found in it.

It brought a signed check with no amount of money defined, it's still yet to be found. It became more of a concern, became a business. People's lives are in jeopardy so let's take advantage of that, they thought. Humans and their dirty minds working their way through pandemic while others were completely terrified of their future.

We've witnessed the craziest period of our existence naked. Completely exposed to a fatal reality and no weapons to kill the enemy. In fact, he was effortless to do its job and kill whoever crossed paths with them. Mentally or physically it was a samurai with a black sword cutting its way through our hopes and dreams, future perspectives and cursing our loved ones' lives with pain, tragedy and a permanent broken heart.

To those surviving, 2020 was certainly doing its job incredible too. Planting a fear seed in their minds, driving them to end a precious journey over something they had never experienced, but were afraid to because it took them everything they could be thankful for. Their minds had tricked them and when they needed themselves the most, they failed on their own rescue. It's too easy when you give advice to others but fail to succeed when it comes to them. How ironic.

A part from that, we better not forget what this year has brought us. Between all its bad stuff, 2020 brought people together. Reminded them that love, peace, not even freedom are granted. That time shouldn't be so strict and there should always be time to love, to make a call, to get together even if it's for a brief moment. 1 minute is enough to tell people how much you mean to them, so why not waste it there instead of making the last invoice of the day?

We didn't have that perception.

We knew that death was certain, life was short and our schedules were even worse. But now we have more time, so even if it's away, don't you think it's time to step up and make up from all the excuses?

With the end of the 2020, 2021 had a difficult task in hand. Bring back hope to people's hearts, a vaccine that might change the end of this story and be better than the one in charge now. Spread love, kindness and hope. Let our hearts light the sky now. It's the only way to get through this: together.

She

*There was a wild flower
in the middle of the desert.
She grew in a world
that wasn't ready for her.
Sand storms, lack of water
and little room to grow.
But she stood tall
and her beauty shined through
the heat of the desert.
She let go some of her seeds
and planted love around her.
Spread kindness and awareness,
inspired others.
And despite the fact
that she still is fighting
for a spot in the sunlight,
she already conquered hearts
and has been noticed.
She is an unfinished poem.
There are lines yet to be written
and some yet to be discovered.
Every verse, every layer
is a piece of her integrity.*

She doesn't stop.
Adding lines and trying new storylines.
Sometimes they might be rough,
not so well written
or not even rhyme between them,
but their beauty will always warm people's hearts.
She is the meaning of love and kindness.
Delicate, stunning, a true piece of heart
If you dare to discover her.
Every layer, every doll is another surprise.
She has some details
That could have been worked a little longer,
but the truth is that without them,
She wouldn't be twice the woman she is today.
A charismatic personality that drives you to do well,
to be a better person.
A loving heart with no boundaries,
a kind soul immune to darkness
and the most caring friend you could ask for.
Golden as the sun.
Deep as the moon. She will make your day better
just by smiling at you.
She is free as a bird,
strong as a stone.
She will never let you down
and always keep your heart warm in the cold.
Her words will hug you,
her writing will inspire you.
She is a beautiful with a stunning soul.
She built her walls with love and kindness.
Little walls turned into high buildings
and those became an empire.
A statement of honesty, respect and strength.

She inspired others to build their path and legacy.
She is an example,
a stunning woman with an amazing character,
and that's the beauty on being a woman.
She is a diamond lost in the middle of a quarry.
Ready to be found but hidden
Between rocks, dust and puddles.
She Shines through the morning sun,
Makes her way up to reach the surface
but it's often buried.
But she doesn't give up,
She Diggs and crawls
and eventually she will make it.
Because diamonds don't go unnoticed.
One day someone will appear,
Clear them up,
help them to work on their flaws
and soon they will realize
how Beautiful they actually are.

Existence

Over my head,
I see the distant stars,
Life is but a whisper,
People come and people go,
Our existence defined by those we know.
Destinies forged as we follow our heart,
Too close to be near,
yet so far apart,
Asleep, when nothing seemed to cross my mind,
Blowing like a leaf in green shadow.
Down the cliff behind the empty house,
The raven croak,
following one another
Into the depth of the night.
When silence passed the space behind,
When conversations echoed dry,
I stopped to contemplate why.
A pointless hollow deep inside
In a field of moonlight between two pines,
I lean back,
as the night darkens and comes on.
I couldn't feel a thing at all.
I woke one day, and simply knew.

Some people battle the darkness with light from within
When all seems lost and there's no end in Sight.
Hiding inside this mind of mine,
Where I once danced imagined moves
Talked with eloquence and of truth
I now sit solemn,
not a sound but screaming thoughts unheard,
aloud where I insipid inside reside,
they will return and will be worn fatigued from battle
with the sea the battle to return to me.
I'm fine. But what does it mean?
A phrase said for years but usually meaning a lie.
A settlement for how something could be?
Or a false testimony for the way that I'm feeling?
I walk and get through each day.
I'm not wounded,
I'm not dying,
I'm just a little lost,
Sometimes I look at myself like a pile of dirt.
And am wondering why am I complaining?
So many people have it worse.
I'm not broken,
I'm just missing a few pieces
but sometimes I just want to run.
I am alive!
I am alive.
My mind no more can disprove than prove
what heart may feel and soul may touch.
Carpe diem they say,
I am glad to be alive,
I am glad to be alive,
I am glad to be surrounded by incredible people,
I am glad to live in comfortable conditions,

I am glad to be able to study,
I am glad to do the things I appreciate.
I am glad.
I am alive.
I am.

CHAPTER TWENTY-EIGHT

Beauty Of Life

You know what's so great about life?

It's the fact that not one person knows the right way to "do" it. The abstruse nature is both the beauty and the downfall.

At the end of the day, there is only one certain thing: you'll always have yourself. Intrinsic satisfaction is the most precious thing a person can have. Live for yourself and for no one else. This year, keep it simple. Happiness is what we seek most.

When you experience a bad day, what's the first thing you do? Perhaps you cry, scream or stress. You may even do a combination of all of the above. If you're anything like me, you tend to feel better for a second, but eventually retreat to feeling foolish for letting a petty problem get to you like that. At the end of the day, you are human.

These feelings that weigh us down are entirely normal. It's the way you get up, the way you then gather yourself, that counts. Be strong because life has a plan for you. A plan that contains many hardships, but is worth all the pain if you make something of it. Do not give yourself the possibility to look back and remember a life of low spirits. Create the life that your grandchildren will sit in awe hearing stories about. The power is yours and yours only.

It is easy to feel that the universe is against you. A string of bad days, they accumulate into a feeling of sorrow and self pity. The trick is, as it always has been, to change your mindset. That is, alter the way you perceive your situation.

I assure you, of the problems you are facing, someone is always going through something even worse and inconceivable to you. Things may be challenging for you, but they are a lot worse for another soul.

Stop crying over what you do not have, and start thanking the world for what you do. Things get better.

All of us have times when we see no hope or light at the end of the tunnel and are close to letting the dark abyss take over. In times like this we must force ourselves to get back up and keep going. Light cannot shine without darkness, and often we need to look a little further to find it. If you were put on this Earth, then you have a purpose by default. Believe in this purpose and realize that you are powerful. The gift of life is yours.

Embrace the present, overcome the hurdles and find the glow of your future. The dark times shape us by giving us our strong personality traits. In the midst of them we feel weak, but once we overcome them we are stronger than ever. Keep fighting. If you didn't have anything to compare the happy days to, you wouldn't know the feeling of bliss.

The reason you know joy from despair is because you have experienced both. One of the things that amazes me about life is how one day, something can consume your every thought, and the next, it can have no meaning. This is both good and bad, depending on the circumstances. It reminds us that feelings of sadness, despair and loneliness will pass eventually. On the flip side, the good times won't last either, so we must truly learn to live in the moment and absorb everything we can while it lasts.

The amount of growth you have had in your life thus far is exponential, yet you probably don't realize just how much development you have undergone as you have missed many moments in life.

To anyone out there, experiencing good or bad: things pass and will soon lose the value they hold currently. Use your senses and take in all you can; give your full attention to what you are doing and appreciate the experience in all its glory. When you feel no hope, remember that there always is. No feeling lasts an eternity and no moment defines a life, so things get better. Live, embrace and experience.

I'm not particularly scientific; formulas and numbers confuse me more than anything else. However, the other day I was reading an article that piqued my interest, and might spark curiosity within you, as well. What many of us don't realize is that the formation of negative thoughts is a complex process that works inside the brain. Groups of genes are turned on and off in a positive or negative way depending on your choices and reactions. These neurological signals get sent from the brain to the body, and what was previously a thought can form into a mental state. There is a physical aspect to thoughts in the way that they are a positive or negative change in your brain cells. This may be eye-opening and confronting, but the good news is that you are in control of this. Naturally, our brains are wired to favour the positive.

We have a natural optimism that exists from day one, so we can change the negativity by wiring the pessimistic thoughts out. Our brains change and grow, which is why a period of mental darkness can be overcome.

The first step to true positivity is the hardest and also the most important; in order to succeed, and I mean wholly and entirely, you have to try to get your mind right.

POETRY SECTION

CHAPTER TWENTY-NINE

Garden Of Life

Consider yourself a flower in the garden of life.
Let sunshine flow through you and sustain you,
with its wisdom and light.
Let its energy feed you and nourish your growth
Let its warmth comfort and surround you,
until your vitality overflows.
Water your thoughts daily with affirmations and kind praise.
Let your spirit be lifted until all negativity is erased.
Nurture the seed of your being with love and you'll flourish.
Invite yourself in,
dig down to your roots to find hope, strength and courage.
Let the flower within you never wither but forever bloom.
Pollinate your mind daily and plant positivity and truth.
Fertilize your heart with the joy and happiness it seeks.
The strength it will bring you will nourish your thoughts
with tranquility and inner peace.
Breathe in the air, let it revive all your senses.
Let it calm you, let it refresh you, let it rejuvenate your defenses.
Tend to your weeds,
pull out the ones that will only hinder your growth.
Speak only kindness, have patience,

allow yourself to be lively and grow.

Surreal Fantasies

dancing moonlight
sleepless nights
my eyes wide open
my mind far away
wandering through
surreal fantasies
that I wish were to be real

Self-Growth

Do you see that woman in front of you?
She's smiling again.
Finally, her self-doubts are fading.
Little by little,
her wounds have been healing.
Look at yourself, girl.
You're blooming and
glowing with self-confidence.
You're no longer that girl
who hid behind the four corners;
You're no longer that girl
who soaked up in tears over unfinished novels;
You're no longer that girl
who chased after for a person whose presence
doesn't even worth their weight on a gold.
Apart from it, you are not your past anymore,
and I am proud of you girl.
You've mended well for the things needed for
goodbyes.
You are now a grown woman
who's strong enough to hold on,
and to let go of things
which only stained the sleeves of your self-affirmation.

Know that you're beautiful,
worthy of love,
and you're worthy of a happy,
and a healthy life.

• 91 •

Shine

you shine so bright
"why do you dim your light?"
looking down at such a exquisite ball of potential
they don't understand
why you wouldn't want to be influential
you deserve the story of your dreams
whispers of a better future call to you

Illuminate

Let your pain
sit out in the sunlight
and let it be engulfed
by the rays of the sun
for the light needs to reach
your darkest corners
and illuminate them all one by one.

Sunset

Explosions of gold and lavender fills the sky;
As the majestic sun bows down and say goodbye.
Curtain of darkness pinned with stars slowly fall,
Overcoming the light of the giant fireball.
Every sunset denotes the end of a day
Completion of a journey on a large display:
Hues of purple and pink so bright, A wondrous sight;
Sad farewell to the light,
warm welcome to the night.
The cycle of days to nights is an endless loop,
Hinting that a day must be solved in one fell swoop.
Cause even if the twilight pledged a day a new,
Seizing every moment seems to be tried-and-true.
Sure as the sunrise, the sun will set in the west.
Same goes to all the things: may it be worst or best.
Everything on Earth will have a sweet downfall;
Certain. Unavoidable. Inevitable.
Fact that everything has its own expiration,
Take nothing for granted: show appreciation.
The things you have today may be gone tomorrow,
Cause time is constantly passing like streamline flow.
But in every sunset we're all given a chance:
To see the ending of a given circumstance,

May not always be tragic, rather, ecstatic,
Since life's 'bout growing, and not being static.
As bright blue sky turns to shade of indigo,
And as the stars and the moon take over the view,
Remember that the night's also temporary;
The coming days may be extraordinary.

CHAPTER THIRTY-FIVE

Sunflower

Vibrant yellow flower on fibrous stalk tower,
Golden ray florets crowned on it's large brown center;
Wearing the color of sunshine and happiness,
Hope, optimism, confidence, and friendliness.
Field of green, filled with thousands of miniature suns,
And with the sound of gentle breeze,
They sway and dance;
Basking under the light of a sunny weather,
Radiating warm, bright, and joyful demeanor.
These sun-shaped flowers sprung up from minuscule
seeds,
Sprouted under the dirt and shadows of the weeds;
Pursued the light of blazing opportunity,
Thus, outgrowing darkness and negativity.
Cause sometimes all we need is light to look up to,
Little ray of promising hope to hold on to,
To step out of the comfort that we are used to,
Or overcome the problems that we're going through.
Since we wouldn't want our one life to be wasted,
We should bloom with grace wherever we are planted
See, there's more to life than just living it: sharing it.
Be a cheery flower that lift someone's spirit.
Be someone's reason to smile when their skies are grey;

Be the sunflower that could brighten up their day;
Simple smile can convey more words than we can say,
Who knows, maybe you could drive those dark clouds
away.
Sunflowers tend to track the motion of the sun,
Starting from the break of dawn till daytime is done;
Then they just face east when they reach maturity,
Convinced that the sun will rise there with certainty.
Truly, sunflower symbolizes steadfast faith;
It doesn't matter if the bright future is late.
It'll look forward to direction of the sunrise,
Hopeful that the next day has blue and cloudless skies.
Since tomorrow's a day we've never seen before,
And no one knows what the future has in the store,
We'll have to hope, believe, and don't stop looking up,
And never give up till the perfect days unwrap.

CHAPTER THIRTY-SIX

Rainbow

Bands of colors painted in the sky saying "Hi";
Creative display after the rainstorm passed by;
Chromatic arch sprinkled with seven-colored dye;
An ephemeral exhibit for you and I.
Splendid display of color, treat for our sight;
Suspended liquid prism dispersing beam of light,
Blended colors separate from the usual white,
Generating array of colorful delight.
The seven colors of the prismatic rainbow:
Starting from the top are red, orange and yellow,
Vibrant colors of green and blue are what follow,
And from below comes violet and indigo.
They say rainbow's a prize for weathering the storm,
Signage of hope posted in colorful art form.
A reminder that after the gloomy downpour,
In the sky will be laid a majestic grandeur.
Like the evanescent beauty of the rainbow,
Happiness can't be permanent, it comes and go;
Yet at the end of the rain - our pain and sorrow,
Colorful hope's waiting just outside our window.
Rainbow's not an object but an experience,
A different view for different audience;
Personal perspective makes all the difference,

To see color in this natural occurrence.
Where does it start or end, that, we can never tell,
Cause rainbows can only be seen on perfect angle;
A colorful display, though it's not really there;
Optical illusion that we can't go over.
So it also means that there is no pot of gold,
In contrary with the stories we have been told,
But there's one thing about it, you can treasure too:
No one experiences a rainbow like you do.
Rainbow is the symbol for happiness and hope,
Something to look up when we're on a downhill slope;
Hinting that there's beauty after the rainiest day,
Greeted and welcomed by multicolored archway.
And of course, we can always choose to be happy,
Find rainbow on what situation we may be;
Believe that sky can be clear, though today's cloudy;
And start to look at our life, positively.

CHAPTER THIRTY-SEVEN

Stars

Glittery and glamorous, lustrous;
sparkly and a speck so mysterious,
far yet still luminous;
How these tiny lights create a sight so wondrous?
It's fabulous!
How they fill the sky so vast, spacious.
Infinite stars which make the night sky glittery;
Scintillating with the excitement they carry;
Though their colors and intensity may vary,
Amidst darkness, it's an inducement to be merry.
Flickering, as if they're dancing at their own beat,
And showcasing their extraordinary feat:
Decorating the heavens with light-speckled treat,
For without them, the night sky would be incomplete.
The stars render the darkest night spectacular:
A sight that is so common, normal, regular;
But with the beauty that's literally stellar,
Makes our every evening unique, dissimilar.
It's the darkest nights that produce the brightest stars:
So, embrace the circumstances that gave us scars;
Own the moments of pain, and the hardships of ours,
So that we can still shine through our most bleak hours.
Sure, we made lot of mistakes that we can't erase,

Yet sometimes wrong choices lead us to the right place;
Making us realize that everything connects,
Like constellations made out of these sparkly objects.
Every speckles in the sky has their own story,
And the darkness of the night enhances their glory;
Though the clouds may sometimes hide the stars from our
sights,
Doesn't mean they're inexistent or out of lights.
So don't think that you're unimportant, trivial;
You are not worthless - you're important, essential;
You are a part of something big, something special;
Don't give up on yourself, you are pure potential.
Humans have looked up to the star for thousand years,
Believing that there's magic in these brilliant spheres;
You may believe it or the science in your shelf,
Still, it's not as fun as believing in your self.

CHAPTER THIRTY-EIGHT

The Chances

The sun glistens over the horizon.
A symbol of dawn,
and a beginning for us to cope,
with its new found hope.
It is another day,
to say, our genuine appreciation.
To stay, and be an inspiration.
To express our deepest regrets,
and to exert an effort,
to amend one's mistakes.
It is indeed another day,
to resume, the unfinished.
To polish one's personality,
and to act upon our wishes,
no matter how slim, the chances.

CHAPTER THIRTY-NINE

Butterfly

Floating gracefully across flowery meadows,
To the colorful flowers, it cheerfully goes;
The pair of chromatic wings, that it proudly shows,
Is like a vivid flower itself, worn as clothes.
Butterflies bring the feeling of joy, happiness,
Their multi-colored wings flutters with loveliness;
Dyed with the color of sunshine, they glide with pride,
From bloom to bloom they guide us to the sunny side.
Butterflies are created from transformation;
They don't emerge as is, but undergo transition:
It's a series of growth, change, and adaptation,
Before it became larger, grander creation.
There are times when we are like a caterpillar,
In development stage - not yet spectacular,
Time when we're still learning, gaining experience,
That would fuel our essence of existence.
Sometimes we envision ourselves, flying high,
A beautiful, colorful, full-grown butterfly,
Skipped essential learning process, we're in a rush,
That we leap before we have wings to carry us.
Sometimes we feel like we are shrouded in darkness,
Forced to retreat as difficulty arises;
We feel alone inside our own chrysalis,

Interpreting that this loneliness' a crisis.
But sometimes this is just time for a break, for rest;
A time to recollect, to bring out our best;
Adversity is vital to build character,
Surely after this isolation, you'll be better.
Cause despite the comfort the cocoon may offer,
We need to emerge from our state of slumber:
We need to let go of the old us to be new,
Transform our perspective, our point of view.
Butterfly can't see their wings from their field of view:
They can't see a colorful fairy, like we do.
So you may not see the beauty that's within you,
Yes, butterflies are beautiful, and so are you.
Everyone has to trust, follow their own process,
Believe that your life is still 'a work on progress';
Just do and give your best to pursue excellence,
And with this, success will chase you, nevertheless.

CHAPTER FORTY

Trails

Trails are nature's awe-inspiring invitations:
Marked foot paths that lead to scenic destinations;
An opportunity to be one with nature,
A chance to capture its features in a picture.
Path that directs to scenic lakes, volcanic peaks,
Roaring waterfalls, calm rivers, and winding creeks,
Green fields speckled with flowers, butterflies and bees,
Mighty mountains, humble hills, and towering trees.
Evergreen corridor of incline and decline,
Brightened through the gaps of leaves by piercing
sunshine;
Trail may be fine as line, but it was by design,
So we and nature may reconnect, realign.
Cause there is no other way to appreciate,
The real beauty of nature and what makes it great,
But to be within it and experience it:
Savor in the sweet ambiance of nature's treat.
Our life's like these enigmatic passageways:
Full of mysteries, and doesn't fail to amaze;
Lots of ups and downs, and intricate like a maze,
Which can only be cherished by living your days.
For it's easier to take life than to live it;
It's easier to give up and quit, than commit;

LOST AND FOUND

It's easier to retreat and accept defeat,
Than to retry and repeat until we make it.
Move consistently to the place you want to go,
Though the steps you can throw may be slow and narrow;
Just move forward and cover a few more distance,
For every moment is a chance to advance.
We can be disheartened by intimidating slopes;
Heavy brush, downed trees, and sharp rocks,
may crush our hopes;
The thought of the unknown may leave you terrified,
But don't let these things stop you from taking a stride.
Cause even though the trails may seem unforgiving,
We must stay on our course and keep on going;
Cherish our life with every breath that we're taking,
And be thankful, for this journey is a blessing.

CHAPTER FORTY-ONE

Sun

A brilliant smile would be great to start a new day,
A warm embrace that comes from far, far away,
A gentle kiss on the cheek by one of it's ray:
The best 'good morning' greeting on a bright display.
'Rise and shine' as the sun pull up its amber sign,
Bringing along bright colorings that's so divine;
Outline of hills and mountains, starting to define,
As the sun brings out its dazzling gold sunshine.
Sunrise marks the journey of the sun in the sky;
After a long night, its a sight for a sore eye;
Warmth and brightness intensifies, as it soar high,
To where astronomical objects usually ply.
Flaring sunlight that can pierce through the thickest cloud,
And it's shinning magnificently, bright and proud;
Sun beams that travel faster than the speed of sound,
Painting colors to everything that is around.
Like sun, never dull your shine for somebody else;
Always listen to yourself and what your heart yells;
You may be shrouded by clouds,
whether thick or thin,
Remember that nothing can dim the light's that within.
When life's cloudy,
always look on the sunny side;

Don't let its shadow stop you from taking a stride;
Reason why you're seeing shadow, there's only one:
You are turning your eyesight away from the sun.
Choose to look at things in a positive manner,
Treat tough situations as chance to grow stronger,
See problems as opportunities to work better,
Use failures as stepping stones to be a winner.
No one has ever hurt their eyes just by looking,
At the brighter and better side of anything;
They say "If you want sunshine, then weather the storm;"
So deal with the situation, not just conform.
Even the sun's weak, when it rises in the morning,
But how it gather its strength, is enlightening.
So, though it's hard to face the problems you're dealing,
You will rise above it all, by persevering.
But how can we rise?
Happy thoughts and pixie dust?
Well, that would be exciting!
That would be a blast!
But what you'll need is, to give yourself a little trust:
Positive disposition that'll yield an upward thrust.
Life may not always be sunshine and butterflies,
Sure, we all have our own personal lows and highs;
And though we're not sure what lies beyond tomorrow;
Still, there are many reason to wake up and rise.

CHAPTER FORTY-TWO

River

River's a watercourse through which freshwater flows,
Starts from the mountains and to the ocean it goes;
Narrow stream at the source that widens through its course,
Carving through the landscapes with it's powerful force.
Water's ceaselessly gushing, always on the move,
Following gradient on earth's predetermined groove;
Usually flows steadily, at times rapidly,
Sometimes peacefully, and frequently noisily.
Well, isn't that the way our lives usually goes?
We're so caught up that we go wherever it flows;
We just follow the meanders, the looping bends,
Drifting along the torrent, the current and trends.
We found insecurities on our identities;
We lose confidence with our own abilities;
We abandon our own individuality,
Just to go along with standards of society.
But shouldn't we be the one deciding where to go?
And maybe know which road we would like to follow;
Or at least dictate the tempo, our rate of flow,
Live and play our life in lento or pianissimo.
Water's soft, fluid, and takes form of container,
Not unless, it is the waters of a river;

For river don't take shape of trenches and valleys,
But forge it's own with persistence that it carries.
Thus, when obstacles on life imposed resistance,
Create new path over time with perseverance;
Gracefully flow at the pace that suits your fashion,
For it takes time to carve a beautiful canyon.
Still, sometimes we let ourselves be taken away,
And 'go with the flow' just as people always say;
In the river of time, we have to move day-by-day,
Well it's okay, guess we can never really stay.
Cause even in the surface it looks calm, tranquil,
Rivers are continuously flowing, never still;
Like constant stream of water that trickle under ,
We'll never take back time that passed between our feet.
But stop thinking that this life's nothing but a race,
Rather, think 'bout things that matter in the first place;
Creating good memory, enjoy life's journey,
With people that are important – friends and family.
River conveys abundance to where it's located,
Likewise, share your life to those whom you're connected,
Cause we're remembered by what we gave, provided,
And not by what we built, attained, nor collected.

CHAPTER FORTY-THREE

Clouds

Skies would only be blue with no clouds on the view:
Both literally and figuratively true;
These soft, light, puffy clouds gives a different hue,
For people who are looking up, like me and you.
Soothing colors of pastel on moving canvas,
Pink, peach, lavender, with little touch from King Midas;
A band of rich palette akin to a rainbow,
Gleaming opportunity for breathtaking photo.
Fluffy feature that'll fade away in the future,
Better catch this colorful mural in a picture:
For this cloud, the elusive floating furniture,
Takes part in sky's ever-fleeting architecture.
Like the clouds, everything in the world is transient,
So let us enjoy the gift of now: the present;
For the past and future are both nonexistent,
Past are now memories, while future's dependent.
We have to concentrate on the present moment,
Can't change the past, but can use it for improvement;
Can't predict the possibilities of future,
Yet, we can still be hopeful for the things we hope for.
Set aside fear and worry, enjoy the journey;
Let the future be present, unhurriedly;
Forget regret, learn from the past, and let it be;

Live in the present, cherish the moment, be happy.
Still, clouds are not always cottony-soft pillow,
At times, dark and heavy like water-filled cargo:
Transporting a torrential and persistent rain,
Blocking the sun like impenetrable curtain.
Then of course we can't always wear a happy face;
But don't worry 'bout rainy days, it's just a phase,
Dark gray clouds will all pass away on its own pace,
Then we'll feel the sun again like a warm embrace.
Remember that beyond these impervious veil,
The radiant sun still shines and will never fail;
Sunshine will then pierce through the thick clouds with it's rays,
Promising us new, sunny and colorful days.

CHAPTER FORTY-FOUR

Moon

It was known that the moon do not shine on its own,
Yet its brilliance is like those of a precious stone;
Reflecting the right amount of light from the sun,
Shinning throughout the night when the long day is done.
Moon shines to make sure our world is bright at night;
A floating lantern, but no fire for its flight;
Pleasurable to watch with its shimmering light,
For the gleam it emits is soothing to the sight.
The surface of the moon is rocky and cratered:
Wrapped in scars, meteor impacts have created;
Still, beauty shine with its blemishes and bruises,
Showing that imperfection glows amidst darkness.
We're meant to shine despite our insecurities,
And ascend beyond our inadequacies;
There may be other stars,
but their light will be dimmer,
If we'll take time to reflect on how we differ.
We just need to own and love our quirks and flaws,
Just by being you alone, deserves an applause.
Be proud of who you are, wear that as a medal;
Cause no one can do 'you' but you, for you're special.
There are nights when we can feel the darkness reigning;
In the sky the cool silvery globe is missing;

But being absent for a while's part of its phasing,
As it follows the cycle of waxing and waning.
For we can never display sparkles all throughout,
There are times we shine all-out, sometimes total blackout;
Cause we can never have all the best in the world,
For those things can not be bottled, packed and be sold.
We are bounded to follow a cycle called life;
Yet it's not as simple as water in a pipe,
For life doesn't just flow where we lead it to go
It's more like a moon-caused tide that goes high and low.

CHAPTER FORTY-FIVE

End Of The Road

Coming to the end of the road,
makes me want to look back,
How much I have done to come this far,
The difficulties I survived,
the harsh words I heard,
the pain that I went through,
But they shaped me to get here, all by myself.
I stop at the end of the road and cry
Realizing this is not what I want,
This is not what I thought of.
Keeping faith and thinking of the bright light after every
dawn,
Going along that long road,
I realized again that you will soon be at the end of the
road,
You just have to be ready for the long road to end.

The End

Thank you for reading
and giving your time.